QUARTER HORSE

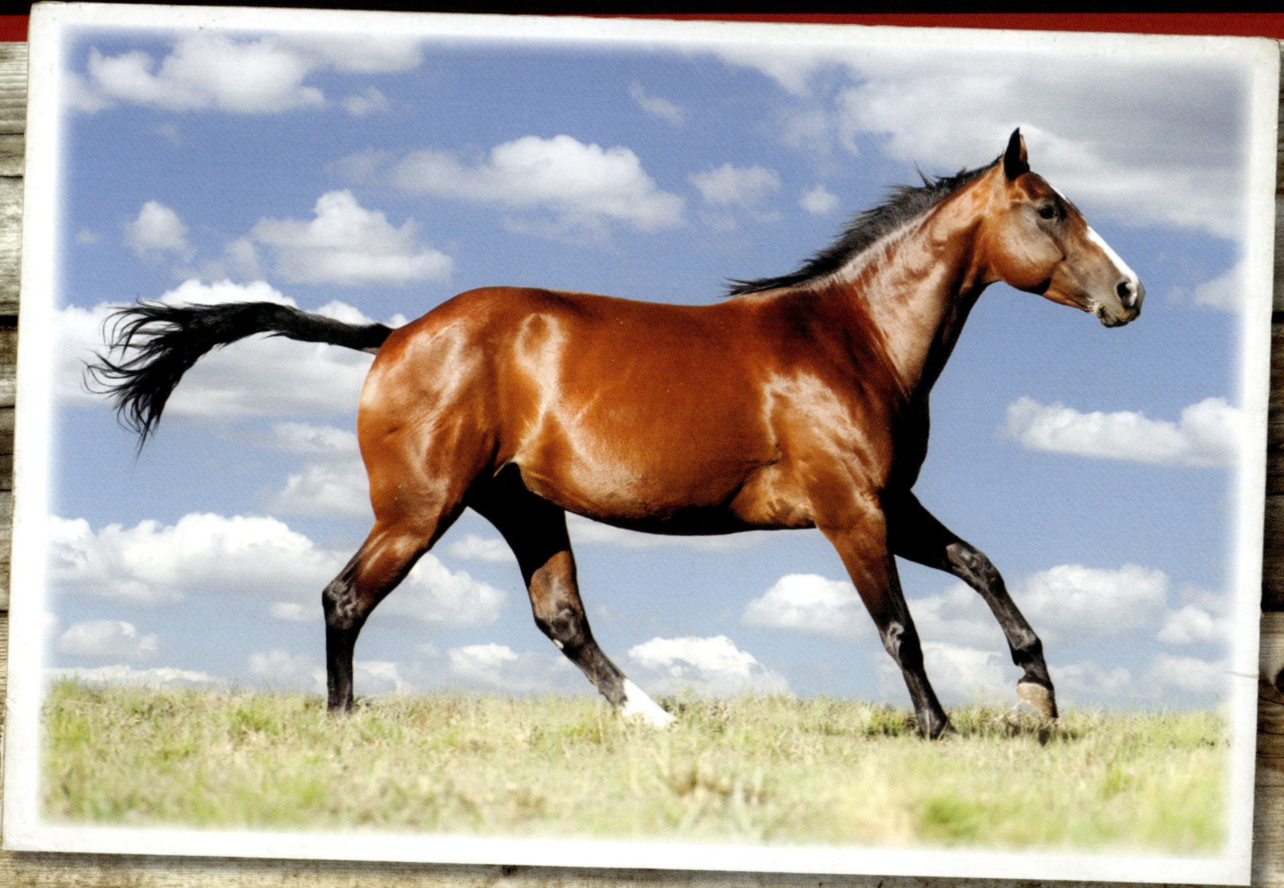

Marylou Morano Kjelle

Creating Young Nonfiction Readers

EZ Readers lets children delve into nonfiction at beginning reading levels. Young readers are introduced to new concepts, facts, ideas, and vocabulary.

Tips for Reading Nonfiction with Beginning Readers

Talk about Nonfiction

Begin by explaining that nonfiction books give us information that is true. The book will be organized around a specific topic or idea, and we may learn new facts through reading.

Look at the Parts

Most nonfiction books have helpful features. Our *EZ Readers* include a Contents page, an Index, and color photographs. Share the purpose of these features with your reader.

Contents

Located at the front of a book, the Contents displays a list of the big ideas within the book and where to find them.

Index

An Index is an alphabetical list of topics and the page numbers where they are found.

Photos/Charts

A lot of information can be found by "reading" the charts and photos found within nonfiction text. Help your reader learn more about the different ways information can be displayed.

With a little help and guidance about reading nonfiction, you can feel good about introducing a young reader to the world of *EZ Readers* nonfiction books.

Mitchell Lane
PUBLISHERS

2001 SW 31st Avenue
Hallandale, FL 33009
www.mitchelllane.com

First Edition, 2021.

Author: Marylou Morano Kjelle
Designer: Ed Morgan
Editor: Morgan Brody

Names/credits:
Title: Quarter Horse / by Marylou Morano Kjelle
Description: Hallandale, FL :
Mitchell Lane Publishers, [2021]

Series: Popular Horse Breeds
Library bound ISBN: 978-1-68020-571-8
eBook ISBN: 978-1-68020-572-5

EZ readers is an imprint of Mitchell Lane Publishers.

Photo credits: Freepik.com, Shutterstock

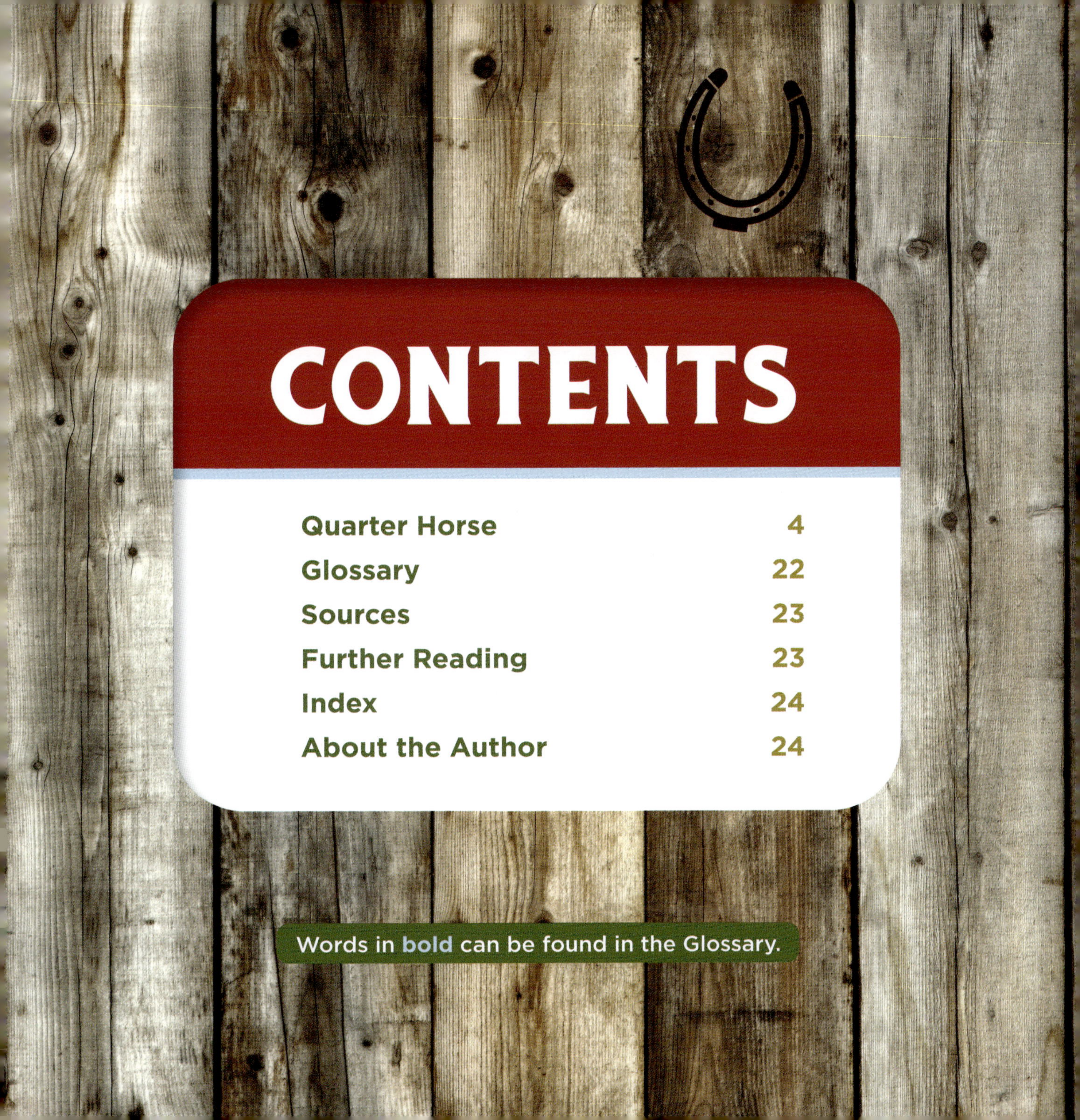

CONTENTS

Words in **bold** can be found in the Glossary.

Quarter Horses are fast horses. They are good at **sprinting** short races.

Did You Know?

Some people believe the Quarter Horse is fast because it has the Thoroughbred Horse in its **pedigree**.

Quarter Horses have wide hips and strong shoulders.

Their head is small. Their eyes are wide. Their **muzzle** and ears are small. Their coats are many colors. The most common color is **sorrel**.

DID YOU KNOW?

Quarter Horses have different facial markings. Common facial markings are blaze, star, snip, and strip.

They eat grass, hay, corn, and oats. Quarter Horses weigh between 1,025–1,250 pounds (465–566 kg). They stand between 14-16 **hands** high.

They live for 25-30 years. A baby horse is called a foal. It takes about 330 days (11 months) for a Quarter Horse to be born.

Did You Know?

The Quarter Horse can **anticipate** the movements of a cow. It is said to have "cow sense." This was helpful to settlers who were setting up ranches in the West in the 1800's.

Quarter Horses are good work horses. They haul lumber. They herd cattle. They clear pastures. They plow fields.

They are good for hunting.

People ride them for fun.

Did You Know?

Settlers used to race the Quarter Horse for a quarter of a mile (0.4 km). This is how it got its name.

Quarter Horses also compete at **rodeo** events.

GLOSSARY

anticipate
Expect or predict

hand
A unit of measure equal to 4 inches, used to measure the height of a horse

lumber
Wood that came from logs cut from trees

muzzle
The nose and mouth of an animal

pedigree
The family history of an animal

rodeo
An event in which people compete at riding horses

sorrel
Reddish-brown in color

sprinting
Running for a short distance

Sources

"American Quarter Horse Lifespan: How Long Do They Live?" *Horsy Planet*. https://horsyplanet.com/american-quarter-horse-lifespan/

Draper, Judith. *The Complete Book of Horses, Horse Breeds, and Horse Care*. London: Lorenz Books, 2007.

Dutson, Judith. *96 Horse Breeds of North America*. North Adams, MA: Storey Publishers, 2005.

Edwards, Elwyn Hartley. *Horses*. London: Dorling Kindersley, 1993.

____________. *Ultimate Horse*. London: Dorling Kindersley, 2002,

Harris, Moira C. *America's Horses: A Celebration of the Horse Breeds Born in the USA*. Guilford, CT: Lyons Press, 2003.

Holt, Bethany G. "The American Quarter Horse." *The Hoof Print*. http://www.equest4truth.com/discover-equus/94-discover-equus/125-american-quarter-horse

"Mare Gestation Calculator." *The Horse*. Thehorse.com.

Further Reading

Web Pages

American Quarter Horse Association
https://www.aqha.com/

Blocksdorf, Katherine. "American Quarter Horse Breed Profile." *The Spruce Pets*.
https://www.thesprucepets.com/meet-the-american-quarter-horse-1886138

Layos, Allie. "Everything You Need to Know About the American Quarter Horse." *Wide Open Pets*.
https://www.wideopenpets.com/all-you-need-to-know-about-the-american-quarter-horse/

Books

Hansen, Grace. *Quarter Horses*. Mankato, Minnesota: Abdo, 2016.

Horses: The Definitive Catalog of Horse and Pony Breeds. New York: Scholastic Inc., 2019.

Jaznyka, Kitson. *National Geographic Readers: Gallop! 100 Fun Facts About Horses*. Washington, D.C.: National Geographic, 2018.

Knoll, Elizabeth, *Quarter Horses (Horse Crazy)*. Mankato, Minnesota: Black Rabbit Books, 2018.

Index

About the Author

Marylou Morano Kjelle lives and writes in Central New Jersey. She is a retired college English professor and the author of over 50 books on various topics for children and young adults. She learned a lot about the Quarter Horse while researching and writing this book. Marylou was especially surprised to learn about the Quarter Horse's "cow sense" and the many other uses for this horse breed.